A MESSAGE TO PARENTS AND TEACHERS:

In this new series of inexpensive books for children, Rand McNally is presenting carefully selected, good literature for the very young child. Books in this series are factual, fanciful, humorous, questioning and adventurous. It is hoped that the series will provide for the masses of children whose parents might be unaware of the availability of good literature at such nominal cost. We firmly believe that the love and appreciation of literature must begin when the child is very young.

This delightful and popular musical game or story as it is presented here needs no explanation as far as its value is concerned. This particular version offers most attractive and colorful illustrations. Discussion of hair color, color of clothing and sizes of children can be encouraged as the verses are read to the young child. Perhaps some appreciation of line, shape and color can be developed also as the pictures are discussed.

The Farmer in the Dell is surely an all-time favorite for home and school. This attractive edition can be read as verse or sung to the familiar tune, enjoyed by one child or a group.

NATIONAL COLLEGE OF EDUCATION
Evanston, Illinois

The Farmer in the Dell

illustrated by Sharon Kane

RAND McNALLY & COMPANY · Chicago
Established 1856

The farmer in the dell,
the farmer in the dell,

Heigh-oh, the derry-oh,
the farmer in the dell.

The farmer takes a wife,
the farmer takes a wife,

Heigh-oh, the derry-oh,
the farmer takes a wife.

The wife takes a nurse,
the wife takes a nurse,

Heigh-oh, the derry-oh,
the wife takes a nurse.

The nurse takes a child,
the nurse takes a child,

Heigh-oh, the derry-oh,
the nurse takes a child.

The child takes a dog,
the child takes a dog,

Heigh-oh, the derry-oh,
the child takes a dog.

The dog takes a cat,
the dog takes a cat,

Heigh-oh, the derry-oh,

the dog takes a cat.

The cat takes a mouse,
    the cat takes a mouse,
Heigh-oh, the derry-oh,
    the cat takes a mouse.

The mouse takes the cheese,
the mouse takes the cheese,

Heigh-oh, the derry-oh,

the mouse takes the cheese.

The cheese stands alone,
the cheese stands alone.

Heigh-oh, the derry-oh,
the cheese stands alone.

The farmer in the dell,
the farmer in the dell,

Heigh-oh, the derry-oh,
the farmer in the dell.